THE
LEWIS & CLARK
EXPEDITION

High Desert Middle School
61111 SE 27th St.
Bend, OR 97702

Essential Events

THE LEWIS & CLARK EXPEDITION

BY SUSAN E. HAMEN

Content Consultant
Professor Robert J. Miller
Lewis & Clark Law School

ABDO
Publishing Company

CREDITS

Published by ABDO Publishing Company, 8000 West 78th Street, Edina, Minnesota 55439. Copyright © 2008 by Abdo Consulting Group, Inc. International copyrights reserved in all countries. No part of this book may be reproduced in any form without written permission from the publisher. The Essential Library™ is a trademark and logo of ABDO Publishing Company.

Printed in the United States.

Editor: Paula Lewis
Copy Editor: Nadia Higgins
Interior Design and Production: Rebecca Daum
Cover Design: Rebecca Daum

Library of Congress Cataloging-in-Publication Data
Hamen, Susan E.
  The Lewis and Clark Expedition / Susan E. Hamen.
     p. cm. — (Essential events)
  Includes bibliographical references.
  ISBN 978-1-60453-048-3
  1. Lewis and Clark Expedition (1804-1806)—Juvenile literature.
2. West (U.S.)—Discovery and exploration—Juvenile literature. 3.
West (U.S.)—Description and travel—Juvenile literature. I. Title.

  F592.7.H255 2008
  917.804'2—dc22

                          2007031210

TABLE OF CONTENTS

Lost in a snowstorm

INTO THE UNKNOWN

In September 1805, a group of explorers made its way through the frigid cold of the Bitterroot Mountains in what are now the states of Montana and Idaho. As snow and freezing rain fell, the group struggled to travel through the steep, slippery mountain passes. The leaders of the expedition, Captain Meriwether Lewis and Captain William Clark, worried they would starve or freeze to death before finding a way out of the mountains.

The group was called the Corps of Discovery. They had been sent by President Thomas Jefferson to explore the uncharted territory the United States had purchased in 1803 from France. Their goal was to travel west from St. Charles, Missouri, to find a waterway that would lead to the Pacific Ocean. The Corps of Discovery was the first expedition of American white men to explore the land west of the Mississippi River—an area occupied by American-Indian tribes. With no maps to guide them, Lewis and Clark relied on Old Toby, a Shoshone Indian, to guide them through the rugged Bitterroot Mountains.

The rain turned to sleet and snow. As the temperatures continued

American-Indian Tribes

In the late eighteenth century, Spain sent John Evans and James Mackay to the area of Mandan, which is in present-day North Dakota. Hudson's Bay Traders had also sent fur trappers into the area.

Lewis and Clark led the first group of Americans into the West. But for a very long time, those lands had been inhabited by American-Indian tribes. The Corps of Discovery came across as many as 100 different American-Indian tribes. Some tribes were friendly and helpful, while others were hostile.

The Mandan and Hidatsa tribes were farmers who built and lived in earth lodges year-round. Other tribes, such as the Sioux, followed and hunted buffalo. They lived in tepees that they could pack up and carry as they migrated in search of buffalo.

to drop, Old Toby lost the trail. The men grew weak from lack of food. Their horses, also suffering from exhaustion and starvation, slipped and fell on mountain trails. Joseph Whitehouse, a member of the expedition, wrote in his journal on September 16, 1805:

> Some of the men without socks, wrapped rags on their feet, and we loaded up our horses and set out without anything to eat, and proceeded on. We could hardly see the old trail for the snow.[1]

Lewis and Clark's Corps of Discovery endured 11 days and 160 miles (258 km) of torturous travel through these mountains before they stumbled out of the wilderness. Weak, injured, and starving, the group found itself in the village of a mighty tribe of American Indians, the Nez Percé. The expedition was hoping to find food, water, and help from the tribe. The explorers did not know, however, whether the powerful tribe of Nez Percé would befriend them or kill them.

A Young Nation

Five years earlier, in 1800, the United States was less than half of its current size. It stretched westward from the Atlantic Ocean to the Mississippi River. France had a claim on the land west of the Mississippi to the Rocky Mountains. This area, called the Louisiana Territory, was mostly unexplored by Europeans and Americans. Only a small number of French fur traders had ventured into the area, but American Indians had been living there for hundreds of years and were entitled to the land.

Not only was the United States much smaller in terms of land size, but approximately only five million people lived in the United States. Two-thirds of all Americans lived within 50 miles (80 km) of the Atlantic Ocean.

THE NORTHWEST PASSAGE

In 1801, Thomas Jefferson became president. He understood the importance of the United States finding a waterway that connected the Atlantic and Pacific oceans. This rumored waterway was called the Northwest Passage. Finding a water passage would mean Americans could transport goods across the country to the Pacific Ocean for trade with Asia.

Jefferson's Passion for the West

Jefferson spent a great deal of time reading and researching about the land west of the Mississippi. Long before he was elected president, he had dreamed of sending a group to explore the land of the Louisiana Territory. Jefferson's personal library at his home, Monticello, held more books about the West than any other library in the world.

This would eliminate the need to sail around the tip of South America or southern Africa.

For many years, England, France, and Spain searched for a passage, believing that whoever found it would control the continent. By the early 1800s, it was believed that no such passage existed in what is now Canada or Mexico. But explorers still hoped to find it in the Louisiana Territory.

Finding such a passage was not the only motive for exploring the West. Jefferson was eager to establish

The Louisiana Purchase

In 1801, France had a claim to the land between the Mississippi River and the Rocky Mountains. This area was known as the Louisiana Territory. It had been handed over to France from Spain on October 1, 1800.

President Jefferson knew the Mississippi River was an important waterway for trade and that New Orleans was a vital port for shipping goods. Jefferson sent Robert Livingston to France to negotiate for the purchase of New Orleans and West Florida. Livingston was authorized to make an offer on the port of New Orleans if the first offer was rejected.

On April 11, 1803, France offered to negotiate not only the sale of New Orleans but also its claim to the entire Louisiana Territory. On April 30, France accepted an offer of $15 million. The Louisiana Purchase gave the United States control of the entire Louisiana Territory.

A Boston Federalist newspaper called the Louisiana Territory,

> a great waste, a wilderness unpeopled with any beings except wolves and wandering Indians. We are to give money of which we have too little for land of which we have too much.[2]

The total land area was more than 800,000 square miles (2,000,000 sq km). The United States paid three cents per acre in a land deal that doubled the size of the country.

fur trapping and trade with American Indians. He believed this would give the United States a better chance to claim the land west of the Mississippi.

MERIWETHER LEWIS APPOINTED LEADER

Jefferson asked 28-year-old Meriwether Lewis to lead the expedition. Lewis was an officer in the U.S. Army and shared Jefferson's desire to explore the land. Jefferson was confident that Lewis was the best man to lead a group into the uncharted territory.

Lewis requested that William Clark be asked to join the expedition. Clark had joined the U.S. Army in 1789. He had experienced several battles with American Indians. He had also served as Lewis's captain in the Army.

Although Clark lacked Lewis's formal education, he was a capable, trustworthy leader. Clark's negotiating skill with the Indians would be useful, as would his skills at drawing maps. Lewis wrote to Clark and asked him to be his cocaptain on the expedition: "… induce you to participate … in its dangers, and honors, believe me there is no man on earth with whom I should feel equal pleasure in sharing them as with yourself."[3] Clark immediately agreed.

DOUBLING THE NATION

While Lewis and Clark prepared for their expedition, Jefferson concentrated on purchasing the port city of New Orleans on the Mississippi River from France. On April 30, 1803, France agreed to sell New Orleans and its claim to the entire Louisiana Territory to the United States for $15 million.

The Man for the Job

Jefferson explained why he chose Meriwether Lewis to lead the Corps of Discovery in a letter to Dr. Benjamin Rush. He wrote, "Capt. Lewis is brave, prudent, habituated to the woods, & familiar with Indian manners & character. He is not regularly educated, but he possesses . . . accurate observation on all the subjects of nature. . . . He has qualified himself for those observations of longitude & latitude necessary to fix the points of the line he will go over."[4]

Although plans for the expedition had been underway before the purchase of the Louisiana Territory, the addition of the large piece of land made the expedition even more necessary. Jefferson, who called the expedition the Corps of Discovery, wanted Lewis to keep journal entries on plants, animals, American-Indian tribes, and maps. Jefferson was eager to learn about the newly acquired land. Meriwether Lewis and William Clark were about to set out on a journey that would change the course of American history.

Meriwether Lewis (left) and William Clark

A full-scale replica of the expedition's keelboat Discovery

PREPARING FOR AN EXPEDITION

In the spring of 1803, Lewis traveled to Philadelphia to study with the American Philosophical Society. He learned about plants, animals, and minerals. He also learned skills such as mapmaking, taking land measurements, and navigating by using the stars. The expedition would not have a doctor with them, so Lewis would serve as the physician. He studied with one of the leading doctors of the time, Dr. Benjamin Rush.

While in Philadelphia, Lewis began making lists of what the Corps would need. He bought maps, tools, food, clothing, compasses, and medical supplies. He bought 15 of the most modern rifles for the time, as well as 420 pounds (191 kg) of lead to be used for bullets and 176 pounds (80 kg) of gunpowder. Lewis also purchased books on botany, mineralogy, and astronomy. The men would need to bring all of the supplies for the trip with them, as there would be no source for supplies in the wilderness.

Lewis knew that it would also be important to have gifts for the American Indians they would meet along the way. The gifts would serve as tokens of peace, as well as items to trade for food. He bought pocket mirrors, rolls of tobacco, ivory combs, brass kettles, beads, and other

Dr. Rush's Advice

While in Philadelphia, Lewis trained with Dr. Benjamin Rush. The doctor instructed Lewis on the importance of wearing flannel next to the skin, especially in wet weather. Flannel was effective in keeping warmth in and disease out. Rush explained, "Flannel shirts worn next to the skin will prevent many diseases. I have known the use of flannel shirts to preserve the health of a whole army. No vermin are bred in it when worn months without washing."[1]

items he felt would be of interest to the Indians. Lewis bought more than 3,500 pounds (1,588 kg) of supplies.

Equipping an Expedition

Lewis had the important task of deciding what supplies the Corps would need on their journey west. Items included:

- maps and compasses
- telescope
- thermometers
- chronometer (for calculating longitude)
- 150 yards (137 m) of cloth for making tents and sheets
- pliers, chisels, and handsaws
- mosquito curtains
- 10.5 pounds (4.8 kg) of fishing hooks and lines
- writing paper and ink
- 12 dozen pocket mirrors
- 4,600 sewing needles
- 144 small scissors
- 10 pounds (4.5 kg) of sewing thread
- silk ribbons
- 130 rolls of tobacco
- 288 knives
- 8 brass kettles
- 33 pounds (15 kg) of tiny beads
- 45 flannel shirts
- coats, shoes, and woolen pants
- blankets
- muzzle-loading rifles
- 500 rifle flints
- 420 pounds (191 kg) of lead for bullets
- syringes and tourniquets
- 6,000 doses of various medicines

BUILDING A BOAT

In the summer of 1803, Lewis made arrangements in Pittsburgh for the construction of a large flat-bottomed boat, called a keelboat. The boat would be used for part of the trip. A keelboat could be rowed with oars or pushed along the river by using long poles. When the river's current was too strong for these methods, the men could pull the boat with ropes while walking along the riverbanks. A sail could be used if the wind cooperated. The boat was 55 feet (17 m) by 8 feet (2 m) and could carry 10 tons (9 tonnes) of supplies. A small cannon, called a swivel gun, was mounted on the front. The keelboat was designed to be taken apart and carried across land if necessary.

The boat was built on the Ohio River. All of the supplies were loaded onto the boat in Pittsburgh. On July 5, 1803, one day after the announcement of the Louisiana Purchase, Lewis set off down the Ohio River toward St. Louis. Clark joined Lewis along the way, and the two spent the journey to St. Louis selecting men to be part of the Corps of Discovery. Lewis and Clark would spend the winter in St. Louis making final preparations for the trip.

Recruiting the Corps

Lewis and Clark knew they needed men who were skilled woodsmen and prepared to be gone for two years or more. Some of the young men they recruited had served in the military; others were French fur traders. Other men had the skills necessary to paddle the pirogues, boats similar to canoes. The final group consisted of 44 men.

The oldest member of the group, 35-year-old John Shields, was a blacksmith. There was also a tailor, a carpenter, and York—Clark's African-American slave since childhood.

The only four-legged member of the Corps was Lewis's dog, Seaman, a Newfoundland that weighed nearly 150 pounds (68 kg). Seaman would prove useful by retrieving squirrels and other small animals the men shot for food. Seaman also served as a guard dog against buffalo that found their way into camp at night.

A Diverse Group

White American military men comprised the majority of the Corps of Discovery, but the group included: men who were French and American Indian, French-Canadian fur traders, and Clark's African-American slave, York. Almost a year into the expedition, a Shoshone woman, Sacagawea, was asked to join the group.

Camp Dubois

The Corps of Discovery spent the winter of 1803–1804 at Camp Dubois, also known as Camp Wood. The camp was located in Illinois, 20 miles (32 km) north of St. Louis on the Mississippi River, and served as a training ground for the men. They built huts and began preparing for the upcoming expedition.

Clark spent the five months at Camp Dubois molding the men into a team. He learned each man's individual strengths. He noted who was good at carpentry, who were the best hunters, and who were especially good at following orders.

Lewis and Clark knew George Drouillard was essential to the expedition. Drouillard was half Indian. His mother was a Shawnee Indian, and his father was French-Canadian. Drouillard was a skilled frontiersman and an excellent hunter. Most importantly, he could communicate with the Indians, as he spoke several Indian languages and knew the sign language of the Plains Indians.

While Clark worked to prepare the men, Lewis secured last-minute supplies in St. Louis. He also spoke with men who had traveled upriver. The fur trappers and explorers gave Lewis an idea of what he could expect to find traveling up the Missouri River to the Mandan Indian villages (present-day North Dakota). Antoine Soulard, who had surveyed Upper Louisiana for Spain, provided Lewis with a map of the Missouri River up to the mouth of the Osage River.

A Wise Addition

Captain Lewis recruited George Drouillard in November 1803. Drouillard proved to be an important addition. Not only was he the best hunter of the party, he also knew the sign language of the Plains Indians. Lewis's journal entry of August 14, 1805 noted, "The means of communicating with these people was by way of Drewyer [Drouillard] who understood perfectly the common language of ... signs which seems to be universally understood by all the Nations we have yet seen."[2]

Lewis also obtained a map of Upper Louisiana and a map made by James Mackay, who had traveled up the Missouri River to the village of the Omaha Indians in 1795.

By May of 1804, outfitted with the supplies and maps, the Corps of Discovery was ready to set out into the unknown. ⌐

Unsavory Soup

Although they packed tons of goods, the expedition ran out of nearly everything. The one supply they did return with, however, was almost all of the 193 pounds (88 kg) of a portable "soup." The soup was a paste made out of boiled beef, cows' hooves, vegetables, and eggs. Even when the group was nearly starving crossing the Bitterroot Mountains in the fall of 1805, no one wanted to eat it.

A pocket compass similar to that used on the expedition

The keelboat Discovery *heads upriver.*

The Exploration Begins

On May 14, 1804, the Corps of Discovery was ready to leave Camp Dubois and head up the Missouri River. The people of St. Louis gathered on the riverbanks to see the men off. Onboard the keelboat, Clark directed the men rowing upstream against the muddy water of the Missouri. Men aboard two pirogues paddled alongside. Lewis, who was still in St. Louis, would meet the expedition six days later upriver at St. Charles.

While in St. Charles, Lewis and Clark added two men to their expedition, Pierre Cruzatte and Francois Labiche. Both men were half American Indian. Cruzatte could speak Omaha and knew the sign language the tribes used. Labiche was able to speak several American-Indian languages.

After three days of rainstorms, the expedition left St. Charles and continued up the Missouri River. They traveled three and one-quarter miles (5.23 km) their first day before making camp on an island. The rain continued, but at 6:00 a.m. on May 22, they were ready to set out.

All in a Day's Work

As the expedition moved westward up the Missouri River, Clark spent most of his time on the keelboat. Lewis walked on shore, studying and taking notes on the animals, plants, and soil. The expedition's best hunters, including Drouillard, also walked in order to hunt for food for the expedition.

Journals

Jefferson had insisted that both Lewis and Clark keep journals of the expedition. The men required their sergeants to do so as well. Lewis and Clark detailed the plants, animals, American-Indian tribes, and daily happenings. These journals help paint a vivid picture of the expedition to the Pacific Ocean.

Lewis remarked about Drouillard in his writings, "I scercely know how we Should Subsist ... was it not for the exertions of this excellent hunter."[1] The men would bring in squirrel, beaver, deer, and turkey.

The boats traveled approximately 14 miles (23 km) per day and sometimes 20 miles (32 km) if the wind was favorable. When the keelboat became stuck on sandbars, the men jumped into the shallow water and pushed the boat free. When the waters were too difficult for rowing, the men pushed long poles into the riverbed and walked from the front of the boat to the back of the boat as they pushed the keelboat against the current. Whether rowing or pushing, moving the keelboat was hard physical work.

On May 25, 1804, the Corps passed a settlement named La Charette—the last area where white people lived on the river. The men of the expedition were totally cut off from the world they knew.

As they continued their journey, the men remained prepared at all times for Indian attacks.

The men made camp on islands whenever possible. In the evenings, they built campfires, cooked their food, made any necessary repairs, and tended to injuries. Guards kept watch at night.

Lewis and Clark had separated the men into three groups called "messes." Each mess had one sergeant. Along with performing assigned tasks, each mess would cook and eat together as a group. They would save a portion of their food to eat cold the next day, as there was no stopping to cook during the day.

PLAGUED BY INSECTS AND ILLNESS

By June of 1804, the explorers were beginning to feel the effects of living in the wild. Gnats, ticks, and mosquitoes were a constant irritation. The swarms were so thick the insects would get into the men's mouths, ears, eyes, and noses. The only remedy was to stand in the campfire's smoke and cover their arms and faces with a mixture of buffalo grease and tallow, called "voyager's grease." At night, everyone slept under mosquito netting.

Very Troublesome Mosquitoes

The men were plagued by mosquitoes. Lewis wrote, "the musquetoes continue to infest us in such manner that we can scarcely exist; for my own part I am confined by them to my bier [mosquito curtain] at least 3/4ths of my time. my dog even howls with the torture he experiences from them ... they are so numerous that we frequently get them in our thr[o]ats as we breath."[2]

The expedition had no fresh fruits or vegetables. The crew ate salt pork, cornmeal, a flour and lard mixture, and fresh meat when the hunters were lucky. They drank murky water from the river. They were unaware that their meat was rancid and the water was contaminated. Soon, many of the men became sick.

Clark's journal entry for June 17, 1804, read, "The party is much afflicted with Boils and Several have the [dysentery], which I contribute to the water."[3] Dysentery is a disease that causes diarrhea and can be fatal if not treated. Some men suffered from heat and sunstroke. Deep in the wilderness, the men had to make do with the treatments Lewis could administer.

Justice on the Journey

On June 26, 1804, the Corps of Discovery completed the 400-mile (644-km) journey by river across present-day Missouri and arrived at the mouth of the Kansas River. On the evening of June 28, the night watchman, Private John Collins, and Hugh Hall decided to sneak some whiskey from the expedition's rations. At daybreak, the two men were discovered and put under arrest.

The expedition held its first court-martial trial. Private Collins was found guilty of being drunk while on guard, and Private Hall was found guilty of taking whiskey without permission. Both men were sentenced to receive lashes with a whip.

INDEPENDENCE DAY

July 4, 1804, one year after the announcement of the Louisiana Purchase, marked the first celebration of Independence Day west of the Mississippi River. The men began the day by firing the cannon. At noon, they pulled over at the mouth of a creek. Lewis and Clark named it Independence Creek.

Medicine and Treatments on the Trip

Captain Lewis served as the Corps' physician. Among their medical supplies, the Corps had 50 dozen of Dr. Rush's pills. These pills were a strong laxative and earned the nickname "Rush's Thunderbolts." Two of the main remedies at the time were purging (by using laxatives) and bloodletting (the process of cutting a person to release blood).

Lewis also used herbs and plants, such as wild ginger, to help with minor ailments. At times, he administered quinine for malaria, laudanum for pain, and sulfur for illnesses.

Men experienced foot injuries, especially while walking across prickly pear cacti that tore their feet. They also endured rattlesnake bites and dislocated shoulders. Among the most common ailments that Lewis treated were malaria and rheumatism (soreness and stiffness in the muscles and joints).

At one point, the "doctor" became the patient. Lewis received gunshot wounds when he was accidentally shot by Pierre Cruzatte while hunting.

Writing and Spelling

Lewis and Clark were excellent at journaling the events of the day as well as the environment, people, and animals they encountered. Their spelling was inventive and inconsistent. For example, they created dozens of ways to spell Sioux. Lewis spelled mosquito at least two dozen ways—none of which was correct. He also spelled United States as Untied States.

In the early 1800s, Noah Webster had taken a personal interest in standardizing the language used by Americans. However, his dictionary was not published until 1806.

That evening, the men camped at a spot Clark described as,

one of the most butifull Plainns I ever Saw ... with hills & vallies all presenting themselves to the river covered with grass and a few scattering trees, a handsom Creek meandering thro.[4]

Each man was given an extra ration of whiskey. They spent the remaining hours of daylight enjoying their drinks and marveling at their beautiful surroundings. At sunset, the men ended the day by firing the cannon again.

THE PLATTE RIVER

By late July, the expedition reached the mouth of the Platte River. They were nearly 600 miles (966 km) into their travels, and the land and animals began to change. The men noticed the trees and grasses were plentiful and lush. The land was abundant with animals of all kinds, and fish were caught in great quantities.

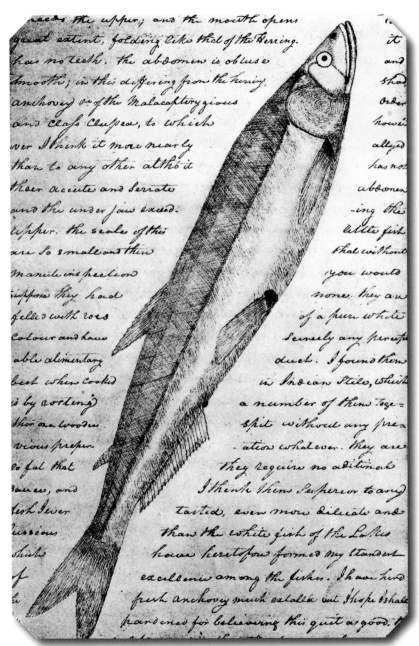

...eeds the upper; and the mouth opens
... great extent, folding like that of the Herring.
... has no teeth. the abdomen is obtuse
... smooth; in this differing from the herring,
... anchovey &c of the Malacapterygious
... and Class Clupea, to which
...ever I think it more nearly
...than to any other altho' it
... their accute and Serrate
... and the under jaw exceed-
... upper. the scales of this
... are so small and thin
... mantle insheeli or
... suppose they had
... felled with roes
... colour and have
... able alimentary
... best when cooked
... is by rosting
... ither on a wooden
... vious preper-
... so fal that
... sauce, and
... fish fewer
... issious
... hich
... of
... it
... and
... shad
... order
... howeu
... alleyed
... has not
... abdomen
... -ing the
... white fish
... that without
... you would
... none. they au
... of a pure white
... scurely any percep
... duct. I found them
... in Indian Stilo, which
... a number of them toge-
... spit without any prepa-
... -ation whatever. they are
... they require no aditional
... I think them superior to any
... tasted, even more dilicate and
... than the white fish of the Lakes
... have heretofore formed my standert
... excellence among the fishes. I have herd
... fresh anchovey much estalled but I hope I shale
... hardened for believing this quit as good.

A sketch of a trout on a page from Clark's journal

Lewis and Clark meeting with American Indians

AMONG THE INDIANS

The country was beautiful and bountiful.
Rivers and streams teemed with fish.
Animals roamed the prairies. As the men explored
the area, however, they had not yet encountered any
American Indians. That would soon change.

On August 3, 1804, a group of 14 Missouri and Oto tribe members met with Lewis and Clark near present-day Omaha, Nebraska. The meeting place was later named "Council Bluff."

With the help of interpreters, Lewis and Clark explained their purpose in exploring the West and the wishes their government had for peace. They told the Indians of President Jefferson, the "great father," who would help them if they promised not to make war with whites or neighboring tribes. As Clark later described in his journals, he and Lewis offered "Some advice to them and Directions how they were to conduct themselves."[1] They presented the Oto and Missouri tribe members with special peace medals, U.S. flags, and other gifts, including gunpowder and a bottle of whiskey. The Corps amazed the Indians with their spyglasses, magnets, and rifles. Captain Lewis fired his air gun, which according to Clark, "astonished those nativs."[2]

The First and Only Loss

In August, Sergeant Charles Floyd became extremely ill. On August 20, he died of what Lewis described as, "Biliose Chorlick" (bilious colic).[3] Most likely, his appendix had burst. In the early

1800s, not even a real doctor would
have been able to save Floyd's life.

The men buried Floyd on a hill
overlooking the Missouri River, close
to present-day Sioux City, Iowa.
Buried with full military honors,
Floyd became the first U.S. soldier
to die west of the Mississippi River.
The Corps honored him by naming
a nearby stream "Floyd's River" and
the hill where he was buried "Floyd's
Bluff." Sergeant Floyd would be the
only fatality among the Corps.

YANKTON SIOUX

Shortly after the meeting with
the Otos, the youngest member of
the expedition went missing. George
Shannon, 18 years old, became
separated from the men while
searching for the Corps' missing
horses. The men searched for several
days but eventually had to continue
on without him.

A Favorite

Lewis found time to study and describe large groups of pelicans, a new animal that he named a "Prarie Wolf" (later known as the coyote), and various aquatic birds. At one point, he had the opportunity to examine a buffalo that had been killed by Private Joseph Field. That night, the men dined on buffalo meat for the first time, and it quickly became their favorite meal.

On August 30, the Corps had a meeting with the Yankton Sioux. Again, Lewis and Clark used an interpreter to speak with the chiefs. The Yankton chiefs agreed to trade with the Americans. They also warned Lewis and Clark about the next tribe they would encounter upriver, the Teton Sioux.

On September 11, Shannon was spotted sitting by the side of the river. After more than two weeks of trying to survive, he decided to wait by the river's edge in hopes that a passing trading boat would find him. Shannon thought he had fallen behind and had hurried to catch up to the keelboat. However, he was ahead of the group. He had survived by eating a rabbit and wild grapes.

The Great Plains

As the expedition continued north and west, the air became drier and trees became more scarce. Lewis noted acres and acres of grassland. They had entered the Great Plains. The men saw coyotes, antelopes, jackrabbits, and prairie dogs for the first time. Immense herds of elk, deer, and buffalo roamed the plains. Pronghorns, the fastest animals in North America, were seen for the first time. Lewis measured, weighed, and described several

The Missouri River was controlled by the Sioux.

new species of animals. He preserved and stored
new plants. The men marveled at the never-ending
rolling hills of grass.

TETON SIOUX

The Corps was especially careful as it entered
Teton Sioux territory in what is now South Dakota.
The Sioux had traded for weapons with British
fur traders in Canada. With those weapons, they

were able to control the Missouri River and the fur trade. The Indians would not want Lewis and Clark reaching neighboring tribes and possibly providing them with weapons.

The Corps encountered the unfriendly Lakota, a band of Teton Sioux Indians, on September 25. The two captains presented their usual speech and demonstration, but the Lakota were not impressed. They demanded more gifts and told Lewis and Clark they would not be allowed to travel any farther up the river.

In order to win over the Lakota, Lewis and Clark invited three of the chiefs onboard the keelboat for a tour and a drink. When Clark took the chiefs back to shore in a pirogue, Indian warriors seized the pirogue's rope. A heated argument arose between one of the chiefs and Clark, who drew his sword. Onboard the keelboat, the men prepared for battle. They loaded the swivel gun and blunderbusses that were mounted to the boat. On shore, Lakota warriors readied their arrows.

It appeared that a battle was about to begin. Chief Black Buffalo calmed the waters by requesting that the tribe's women and children also tour the keelboat before the expedition moved upriver. The meeting had not been successful, but a battle had been avoided. The Corps of Discovery spent three uncomfortable days with the Lakota until they set off up the Missouri River.

BEFRIENDED BY THE MANDAN AND HIDATSA

In October, the keelboat was moving north up the Missouri River. The days grew shorter and colder, and soon snow fell. When the Corps entered present-day North Dakota, they had traveled 1,600 miles (2,575 km). Near the mouth of the Knife River, about 50 miles (80 km) north of what is now Bismarck, North Dakota, the expedition arrived at the Mandan and Hidatsa villages, five earth-lodge villages within a few miles of one another.

The Buffalo Hunts

Lewis and Clark's men accompanied the Mandan on buffalo hunts. The men were impressed by how the Indians were able to ride their horses bareback while shooting arrows at the stampeding herds.

The group of nearly 4,500 Hidatsa and Mandan were farmers and did not move around as other tribes did. Instead of tepees, they built permanent earth lodges and lived peacefully with each other. The two tribes hunted buffalo for meat and hides. They traded with other tribes as well as British, French, and Spanish traders.

An earth lodge

The Hidatsa and Mandan tribes were eager to trade with Americans as well. The Indians were hoping to acquire metal goods and rifles. Hidatsa Chief Black Moccasin and Mandan Chief Black Cat and Chief Sheheke became friends with Lewis and Clark. The two tribes welcomed the Corps of Discovery, who set up their winter quarters on the banks of the Missouri River across from the Mandan villages.

Surviving the Winter

The Corps of Discovery endured freezing temperatures at Fort Mandan during the winter of 1804–1805. Often, it was too cold to go outdoors to hunt for food. Several men suffered from frostbite while hunting.

The men had to look for other ways to find food. They established a trading system with their neighbors, the Mandan. John Shields and Alexander Willard performed blacksmithing services and made battle axes in exchange for corn. Even with the corn received in trade, Lewis and Clark worried about food.

FORT MANDAN

The Corps began building a wooden fort they called Fort Mandan. The walls were 18 feet (6 m) high. Inside the fort, eight huts served as sleeping quarters, a guardroom, a blacksmith shop, and storehouses. The days grew colder and the men fought freezing temperatures and frostbite as they worked to complete the fort. Clark wrote in his journal on December 12, "we do not think it prudent to turn out to hunt in Such Cold weather."[4] The night of December 17 brought a temperature of -45 degrees Fahrenheit (-43°C).

The fort was completed by Christmas Eve. The men celebrated New Year's Eve with the Mandan. Pierre Cruzatte played his fiddle, and the Indians marveled at the music and Clark's slave, York. Some Indians had come into contact with whites before, including French-Canadian fur traders, Spaniards, or

British. But none had seen an African American before. Some tried to rub the color off of York's skin, thinking he was a painted white man.

SACAGAWEA

In 1801, Sacagawea, which meant "Bird Woman," had been kidnapped by the Hidatsa, who took her back to their village. She was then sold to a French-Canadian fur trapper named Toussaint Charbonneau. Sacagawea became his wife.

Lewis helped treat the 17-year-old Shoshone, Sacagawea, who was having difficulty

Sacagawea

Sacagawea was the only female member of the Corps of Discovery. Her presence on the trip was an asset to the Corps. They came into contact with several new tribes, some of whom had never seen white people before. On October 19, 1805, Clark wrote,

> ... the sight of This Indian woman, wife to one of our interprs. [interpreters] confirmed those people of our friendly intentions, as no woman ever accompanies a war party of Indians in this quarter.[5]

In addition to calming the suspicions of the American Indians, Sacagawea also proved to be skillful at digging up edible plants as well as making moccasins and clothing. Lewis and Clark named a river after Sacagawea—Bird Woman's River—because her name means "Bird Woman" in Shoshone.

At the end of their trip, Charbonneau was given $500.33 and 320 acres (129 ha) of land. Sacagawea received nothing.

In the years since the Corps of Discovery, Sacagawea has been honored with statues, monuments, and stamps. In 2000, the U.S. Mint introduced the Sacagawea dollar coin, a gold-tinted coin depicting Sacagawea and her baby, Jean-Baptiste. In 2001, she was posthumously made an honorary Army sergeant.

giving birth to her baby. Lewis had heard of a remedy that could ease labor pains. He ground the rings of a rattlesnake into a powder, mixed it with water, and gave it to the young mother. On the night of February 11, 1805, Sacagawea delivered a boy. Charbonneau named the baby Jean-Baptiste.

In the spring, Lewis and Clark hired Charbonneau and Sacagawea as interpreters. The captains hoped to be able to communicate with the Shoshone tribe to trade for horses in order to cross the Bitterroot Mountains. Lewis and Clark came up with an elaborate plan. Sacagawea would communicate with the Shoshones and translate the conversation into Hidatsa. Charbonneau would translate the Hidatsa into French. Finally, Labiche would translate the French into English for Lewis and Clark. It was the best—and only—plan they had.

A depiction of Sacagawea with Jean-Baptiste in a cradleboard on her back

The expedition continues westward.

WESTWARD BOUND

The men had endured a bitterly cold winter. Now the thick river ice had broken off enough that they could continue their expedition. On April 7, 1805, it was time to leave the friendly Mandan and Hidatsa and continue the journey westward. But not everyone would be heading west.

During the winter months, Lewis and Clark had prepared items for the return to St. Louis. These items were gathered for the journey back aboard the keelboat to St. Louis and on to President Jefferson. Lewis sent a long report detailing the Missouri River and all its tributaries the Corps had passed. Clark included an account of the Indian tribes they had encountered.

Corporal Richard Warfington was put in charge of the small group of men returning to St. Louis. On board the keelboat were six soldiers and two Frenchmen. Alongside the keelboat, two French hunters paddled a canoe. Warfington would lead the group through Sioux territory. Because the keelboat carried such precious cargo bound for the president, Captain Lewis instructed Warfington to be on the lookout for

Precious Cargo

The keelboat traveled back to St. Louis with news from the Corps, as well as animal and plant specimens. Lewis and Clark had also included their detailed journals and maps that they had drawn.

The cargo would offer President Jefferson his first glimpse at some of the things the Corps of Discovery had encountered. Several fur pelts were sent, along with bones and skeletons from animals such as the white and grey hare, a mule deer, antelope, and prairie dogs. Horns from bighorn sheep, elk, and deer also made the journey to St. Louis. The boxes also contained articles of Indian dress, along with a Mandan bow and quiver of arrows, some Aricara tobacco, and an ear of Mandan corn.

Live animals were sent back as well. A prairie dog, four magpies, and a prairie hen began the journey, but only the prairie dog and one magpie would survive the trip.

Sioux and to shoot his way through if necessary.
With the keelboat heading downriver to St.
Louis, 33 members of the Corps of Discovery
would continue the expedition. Four civilians accompanied the expedition: Drouillard, Charbonneau, Sacagawea, and Jean-Baptiste, who was not quite two months old.

Mapping the Expedition

Jefferson had asked Lewis and Clark to take careful observations of latitude and longitude. In order to correctly calculate the two, the captains relied on the stars and mathematical equipment, including the chronometer and an octant or sextant.

The men used a chronometer, which is a very accurate clock, to determine longitude. Earth completes one full rotation (360 degrees) every 24 hours. Therefore, a specific geographic point moves 15 degrees in one hour. Even though the chronometer was wound daily, it still would stop unexpectedly at times. This led to flaws in measurements. A mistake of two degrees amounted to approximately 100 miles (161 km). It could take weeks of paddling and walking to correct this error, time that would deplete the men's energy and supplies.

Latitude was determined by an octant or a sextant to measure the angle between the North Star and the horizon. Latitude readings based on these instruments were very accurate.

Lewis and Clark also used a compass for determining directions. The men estimated distances from one point to another by eye. When they wanted more accurate measurements, they used a two-pole chain, which measured 33 feet (10 m) in length.

INTO MONTANA

Captain Clark led the expedition upriver. Lewis decided to walk on shore the first day. The Hidatsa Indians had forewarned the Corps about the land, the river upstream, and a mammoth waterfall. Lewis and Clark were heading into territory that had never been explored by white men. Lewis estimated his expedition would reach the Pacific Ocean by summer and be back to the Missouri River by winter. In his report to President Jefferson, he had written, "You may therefore expect me to meet you at Monachello [Jefferson's house, Monticello] in September 1806."[1]

The group passed the mouth of the Yellowstone River in what is now North Dakota by the end of April. As they traveled into the Great Plains of present-day Montana, Lewis noted, "We saw immence quantities of game in every direction around us ... herds of Buffaloe, Elk, and Antelopes with some deer and woolves."[2]

Each man consumed up to nine pounds (4 kg) of buffalo meat every day. On May 6, 1805, Lewis wrote in his journal, "It is now only amusement ... to kill as much meat as the party can consum; I hope it may continue thus ... but this I do not much expect."[3]

Beaver were plentiful and the most prized. Beaver tail quickly became the favorite meal. The fur pelts were saved to be returned to the East, where they would fetch a handsome price.

Sacagawea contributed to the expedition's meals by scouting for root vegetables, such as wild artichokes. She also helped set up the tepee the captains slept in at night, along with Charbonneau, herself, and her baby. She traveled the many miles with Jean-Baptiste strapped to her back.

THE DREADED GRIZZLIES

On April 29, the explorers had their first encounter with a grizzly bear. As Lewis and another man walked along the shore, they saw two grizzlies and fired at them. Both bears were hit—one escaped, and the other charged Lewis. Luckily, the men were able to reload their weapons and shoot the bear.

The Indians had warned the men about the grizzlies. But Lewis believed that since the Indians pursued the bears with bows and arrows that the Indians "may well fear this anamal ... [but] in the hands of skillfull riflemen [the bears] are by no means as formidable or dangerous. . . ."[4]

On May 5, however, Lewis learned how ferocious a grizzly bear could be. The men encountered a larger bear, which took ten shots to bring down. Lewis's journal entry described a "tremendious looking anamal, and extreemly hard to kill."[5]

Attacked by bears

The men endured several encounters with grizzlies as they moved through Montana. At times, some men were forced to jump in the river to escape an enraged bear. This gave the other men time to reload their rifles. Dealing with the ferocious bears soon lost its excitement.

A Close Call

The men also dealt with other dangers. On May 14, a particularly windy day, as Charbonneau and

Cruzatte paddled against high waves, the pirogue began taking on water. Charbonneau lost control of the vessel as Lewis watched helplessly on shore. The pirogue carried their scientific instruments, navigation tools, journals, medicine, and maps. While Charbonneau panicked, Cruzatte was able to save the pirogue, although many items were washed overboard. Sacagawea grabbed most of the items from the water and saved everything except for some seeds, a small amount of gunpowder, and some cooking utensils.

Naming Technique

As the Corps discovered new rivers, they were named after members of the expedition. Once every man had a river named after him, they named the waterways after loved ones.

WHICH FORK TO TAKE?

The expedition pushed on. On May 26, 1805, Lewis caught his first glimpse of the Rocky Mountains. He saw the snow on the mountain peaks and recognized that the Rockies would be a challenge.

On June 2, 1805, the expedition came upon a fork in the Missouri River. The group was forced to make a decision about which route to take. Lewis and Clark knew they would waste valuable time should they choose the wrong route and have to double back. The captains felt the south fork was the Missouri. Their men disagreed, arguing the other fork must be the Missouri.

The captains had been forewarned by the Hidatsa about the great falls. They knew whichever river led to a great waterfall had to be the correct way. After scouting the two waterways, the men decided to take the southern fork. Lewis named the other fork the Marias River. As the men began paddling down what they believed to be the Missouri River, Lewis went ahead of the others on foot to scout for the falls.

The Great Falls

The Corps had chosen the correct fork. On June 13, Lewis came upon the Great Falls of the Missouri River. He watched the water crash at the bottom of what appeared to be an 80-foot (24-m) drop. He walked on and discovered four additional waterfalls. The men would be forced

Caching

When the expedition reached the mouth of the Marias River, Lewis and Clark decided to lighten the load by building a cache, or storage space, for one of the two pirogues and a good deal of the baggage. They dug a large hole in the ground and deposited the blacksmith tools, some axes, files, two kegs of pork, salt, two rifles, and other supplies. Lewis branded the surrounding trees to mark the territory. He planned to retrieve these items on the return trip to St. Louis.

to portage on land around the water for 18 miles (29 km) to get around the dangerous falls.

Lewis reunited with the men at a place they named Portage Creek. They cached, or stored, the second pirogue and some of the supplies. Next, they built carts from the few cottonwood trees they could find. Hauling six canoes and all the cargo in blistering heat, they began the backbreaking 18-mile (29-km) trip. They endured rattlesnake bites and peach-sized hail. Grizzly bears tormented the group, but the men pressed on.

By early July, the Corps had completed the portage. They celebrated their second Independence Day by feasting on beans, dumplings, and buffalo meat. They danced as Cruzatte played his fiddle.

Lewis and Clark were behind schedule. They had predicted the portage would take only half a day—not an entire month. Lewis knew his prediction that they would reach the Pacific Ocean and return to the headwaters of the Missouri by winter would never happen. They still had the Rockies to pass—the likes of which none of them had ever seen before. ⌒

Lewis at Great Falls

Looking down from the Continental Divide

CROSSING THE
CONTINENTAL DIVIDE

s the Corps of Discovery paddled onward, they discovered they were not traveling west toward the Continental Divide, but instead were traveling south. After days of navigating the river, they paddled their canoes through a narrow canyon Lewis named the Gates of the Rocky Mountains. Majestic cliffs, approximately 1,000-feet (305-m) high, rose up on both sides as they passed through the canyon and on to a plain surrounded by distant mountains. Sacagawea recognized the place and assured the men they were getting closer to her people, the Shoshone Indians.

On July 25, 1805, they reached the Three Forks of the Missouri River, which is where the Missouri splits into three rivers. They named one of the three rivers the Jefferson River. The other two were named after the Secretary of State James Madison and the Secretary of the Treasury Albert Gallatin.

By Clark's estimates, the Corps of Discovery had traveled 2,500 miles (4,023 km) since leaving St. Louis. In order to continue, it was vital they find the Shoshone tribe to obtain horses to carry them over the mountains. Sacagawea assured the captains they were close to the place where she had been taken captive five years earlier. Still, they had not seen any Indians. They had no choice but to continue.

STRUGGLING UP THE JEFFERSON RIVER

The expedition continued up the Jefferson River, heading west against a swift current. The men pulled the canoes by rope. They slipped on the rocks of the river bed, endured prickly pears, and were tormented by mosquitoes and gnats.

Food to Fuel an Expedition

Food varied by location. East of the Rockies, wild game was plentiful and the men consumed large amounts of meat, including buffalo, elk, beaver, deer, and bear. But when the Corps ascended into the Bitterroot Mountains, game was so scarce that they nearly starved. On the journey between the Rockies and the Pacific Coast, fish and roots were the main source of food. This diet caused indigestion for most of the men. They opted to eat dogs they received in trade from the Indians. Without a doubt, the men preferred meat.

Their food could be divided into three categories: food they purchased and brought with them; food they found along the way, such as meat and wild fruit and berries; and food they obtained through trade with the American Indians.

Before the trip, Lewis had purchased and packed 45 kegs of pork, 50 kegs of flour, and 18 kegs of whiskey. They had also brought lard, coffee, sugar, corn, and beans. Along the trail, they were able to gather fruits such as cherries, gooseberries, strawberries, grapes, pawpaws, and currants.

The men tasted a wide variety of animals during their expedition. These included: porcupine, antelope, cougar, wolf, horse, whale, eagle, quail, hawk, pelican, vulture, and swan.

While working their way up the Jefferson River, the Corps ran into other problems. Several small streams forked off the Jefferson River. At times, the Corps took the wrong waterway and had to turn back. Some of the men were sick, and Clark battled a painful tumor on his ankle that made walking nearly impossible. The expedition continued in spite of these setbacks.

On August 8, near present-day Dillon, Montana, Sacagawea recognized a high rock outcropping on their right. It was Beaverhead Rock. This confirmed they were on the right waterway and close to the Shoshone Indians. Both captains led search parties in hopes of finding the Shoshones, but still they had no luck.

The next day, Lewis, Drouillard, and two other men set out on foot ahead of the others—determined to find the Indians and the horses. They searched for the point at which the Missouri River came out of the mountains. On August 11, after walking five miles (8 km), Lewis caught sight of a Shoshone on horseback. He later wrote in his journal,

> I was overjoyed at the sight of the stranger and had no doubt of obtaining a friendly introduction to his nation provided I could get near enough to him to convince him of our being whitemen.[1]

As Lewis slowly approached the Shoshone, he signaled that he was a friend and not an enemy, but the Indian turned his horse around and was gone. Lewis wrote, "I now felt quite as much mortification and disappointment as I had pleasure and expectation at the first sight of this indian."[2]

Reaching the Continental Divide

The next day, Lewis and his group of men walked up a gentle slope and found a small stream—the headwaters of the Missouri River at Lemhi Pass. Drinking from the ice-cold water, the men rejoiced. They had found the beginning of the mighty river they had been battling for more than a year.

The men continued their hike up the ridgeline, anticipating standing on the Continental Divide. As Lewis climbed the last few feet to the top of the ridge, he expected to look down over the western side of the mountain and see a gentle slope followed by a plain of rolling green land. When Lewis reached the top, however, there were no gentle slopes or rolling green hills. He saw nothing but endless snowcapped mountain peaks. His journal entry described "immence ranges of high mountains still to the West of us, with their tops partially covered with snow."[3] Lewis and the small group of men with him that day realized their hopes of finding the Northwest Passage were over. It seemed as if there was no water route connecting both coasts.

Continental Divide

The Continental Divide is a ridge of the Rocky Mountains. It separates the direction in which rivers in North America flow. Water that flows west of the Continental Divide runs into the Pacific Ocean. Water flowing east of the Continental Divide eventually runs into the Atlantic Ocean or the Gulf of Mexico.

Lewis's journal mentions nothing about his feelings as he gazed at the endless range of mountaintops.

As Lewis looked at the peaks of the Bitterroot Mountains, he realized how important it was that they find the Shoshone Indians and secure horses. The journey to the Columbia River, which would lead them to the Pacific Ocean, would be a treacherous one. They would not make it without horses. Determined to continue, he stepped over the Continental Divide and descended the steep ridge into present-day Idaho. Soon he came across "a Creek of cold Clear water. here I first tasted the water of the great Columbia river."[4]

The four men made camp ten miles (16 km) down the mountain. They were a few days' hike from Clark's group. And most likely, the Shoshone Indian Lewis had encountered was warning his tribe of strangers. Lewis needed to find the Shoshones quickly and make his peaceful purpose clear to them.

Help from the Shoshones

The next morning, Lewis and his men rose early. They followed a heavily traveled Indian path down the valley, where they came upon an elderly Shoshone woman and two girls. The older girl fled, but the old woman and the younger girl stayed where they were and held their heads down, as if prepared to die. Lewis approached, rolled up his shirtsleeve and showed them his white skin. His men presented beads, vermilion paint, and small mirrors. With the help of Drouillard, who used his sign language, Lewis asked the elderly woman to take them to her chief.

After a short distance, they were surrounded by 60 warriors on horses. The Shoshones could have easily overtaken the four men. Lewis laid down his rifle and raised the American flag. He followed the elderly woman, who showed the chief the gifts Lewis had given them. The chief dismounted his horse, approached Lewis, and placed his left arm over Lewis's right shoulder. Pressing his cheek against Lewis's, the chief said, "ah-hi-e" repeatedly, which meant "I am much pleased."[5] Chief Cameahwait led Lewis and the others back to his camp.

The Shoshones

Lewis studied the Shoshone tribe and wrote about them in great detail in his journal. He described them as "deminuitive in stature, thick ankles, crooked legs, thick flat feet."[6] Most of the men and women had short hair. It was their custom to cut their hair while in mourning, and many had lost tribesmen during the raids by the Blackfeet Indians.

Shoshone daughters were sold to be wives while they were still infants. They were given over to their husbands when they turned 13 or 14. Sacagawea's father had sold her as a child, and her intended husband was still among the tribe. But, seeing that she had a husband and a child, the young Shoshone relinquished his claim on her.

The Shoshone Indians had suffered greatly at the hands of the neighboring Blackfeet tribe and were left with very little. But they were willing to share what food they had with the Americans. Through Drouillard's sign language, Lewis conveyed his hope to trade weapons for horses. Lewis asked Cameahwait to meet Clark and the rest of the men at Lemhi Pass. He also asked if the Shoshones would help the Corps bring their packs and supplies down the western side of the mountain.

The next day, Cameahwait's warriors refused to go. They were certain they were being led into an ambush. Lewis told them that they needed to go in order to bring the white men who had the weapons and ammunition for trading. The men proceeded but were skeptical.

The next day, August 17, 1805, the two groups of Americans were reunited. The days of dragging the canoes were over.

HOMECOMING

Lewis and Clark negotiated for horses with the Shoshones. They began the process of translating through several languages. Soon after they began, though, Sacagawea recognized Cameahwait as her

brother. After more than five years, brother and
sister were reunited. Lewis and Clark were able to
negotiate for the horses they needed to continue
their mission. Their camp became known as Camp
Fortunate.

On August 18, 1805, the day of Captain Lewis's
thirty-first birthday, the men portaged their supplies
up and over Lemhi Pass to the Shoshone village.
Lewis's journal entry for that day was a bit reflective.
He hoped to "live for *mankind,* as I have heretofore
lived *for myself.*"[7]

Lewis and Clark gave gifts of beads, knives,
and other trinkets to the Shoshone people in
appreciation of their kindness and help. They
presented Cameahwait with a special peace medal.
It had an image of Jefferson on one side and the
clasped hands of an Indian and a white man on the
other. They also gave Cameahwait a uniform coat,
leggings, and tobacco.

With horses packed and ready, the Corps of
Discovery was about to begin the long journey across
the mountains. Sacagawea said good-bye to her
people, as she, Charbonneau, and Jean-Baptiste
continued on with the Corps. ⌐

An American Indian in the Rocky Mountains

Rugged terrain on the Lolo Trail

CROSSING THE MOUNTAINS

When the Corps of Discovery left the Shoshone village on September 1, 1805, they had one new member. Old Toby, a Shoshone, agreed to help guide the Corps across the Bitterroot Mountains. The Nez Percé Indians used the Lost Trail Pass to cross the mountains on their way to the Great Plains for buffalo hunts. The going was rough. Clark wrote,

> *thro' thickets in which we were obliged to Cut a road, over rockey hill Sides where our horses were in [perpetual] danger of Slipping to Ther certain distruction & up & Down Steep hills ... with the greatest dificuelty ... we made 7½ miles.*[1]

On September 3, snow fell, and the night brought freezing temperatures. The next day, the group came across a band of friendly Salish Indians by a river Lewis named Clark's River. The Salish were generous and willing to sell and trade horses. Lewis and Clark added 13 horses and traded some of the Shoshone horses for better ones. The Corps now had 39 horses, 3 colts, and a mule.

The group headed north, following the Bitterroot River. They covered 66 miles (106 km) from September 7 to 9. The men saw the snow-capped peaks of the Bitterroot Mountains to the west. Sergeant Patrick Gass wrote that the mountains were "the most terrible mountains I ever beheld."[2] The explorers knew they would have to

> "The mountains to the East Covered with Snow. ... This day we passed over emence hils and Some of the worst roade that ever horses passed, our horses frequently fell."[3]
> —*William Clark,*
> *September 2, 1805*

cross those mountains. They made their camp, which they called Travelers' Rest, where the Lolo Creek ran into the Bitterroot. From here they would turn west and begin their climb up and over the mountains. During their two-day stay, they prepared for their ascent into the mountains.

ON THE LOLO TRAIL

The Corps began their trek into the Bitterroot Mountains on September 11. They followed the Lolo Trail, an Indian path, through the mountains. They were running out of food, and there was little game to hunt. Other hardships soon followed. On September 14, the Corps endured rain, hail, and snow, and Old Toby became lost. That night, when the hunters came back empty-handed, the men killed one of their colts for food.

The next day was difficult, too. The horses struggled along the rugged trail and climbed a steep, slippery ridge. Clark's horse fell and rolled approximately 120 feet (37 m). Fortunately, the horse was not injured. The party made only 12 miles (19 km) that day. Their only meal consisted of melted snow and what was left of the butchered colt. And things were about to get worse.

DESPERATION

On September 16, more snow fell before the party awoke. As the group struggled on the trail, Clark traveled ahead of them working hard to find the trail in the six to eight inches (15 to 20 cm) of new snow. The explorers were exhausted. Without grass, the horses were near starvation.

Lewis and Clark knew the situation was desperate. The men were starving and the food was gone. Sacagawea was carrying Jean-Baptiste through the treacherous terrain and cold, wet weather. As much as they hated to split up, the captains decided Clark would take six men and go on ahead to search for a way out of the mountains.

Starving, exhausted, and quickly losing hope, the Corps of Discovery had no choice but to press on led by Lewis. Some of the men became sick with dysentery. They all grew weaker from malnutrition.

OUT OF THE BITTERROOTS

Lewis's group came upon an open area of prairie land on September 21. Finally, the horses were able to graze. The following day, they found "the greater

> "... began to Snow about 3 hours before Day and continued all day the Snow in the morning 4 inches deep on the old Snow, and by night we found it from 6 to 8 inches deep, ... I have been wet and as cold in every part as I ever was in my life."[4]
> —*William Clark, September 16, 1805*

"Capt. Lewis scercely able to ride on a jentle horse which was furnished by the Chief, Several men So unwell that they were Compelled to lie on the Side of the road [trail] for Some time others obliged to be put on horses ... Lewis verry sick ... most of the Party Complaining."[6]

—*William Clark, September 24, 1805*

part of a horse which Capt Clark had met with and killed for us."[5] Lewis and the others feasted. The Corps of Discovery had made it out of the Bitterroot Mountains alive. They had endured 11 grueling days in the mountains and traveled 160 miles (257 km) from Travelers' Rest.

On September 22, the two groups were reunited. Clark sent Private Reubin Field to meet Lewis and the others. Field brought dried fish and roots. He also informed Lewis that his group had found the Nez Percé Indians, who had been friendly.

AMONG THE NEZ PERCÉ

Private Field led Lewis's group to the first of two Nez Percé villages near present-day Weippe, Idaho. Clark, who had been at the second Nez Percé village gathering information for his journals, joined them that night. Clark found them eating camas roots. Clark warned them that eating too much of the vegetable would make them sick, as they had been eating only meat for months. Starved for food, the men did not heed his warning. The next day, many became violently ill with diarrhea and vomiting.

One of the Nez Percé chiefs, an older man named Twisted Hair, drew a map of the land to the west on an elk skin. The map detailed the creek they were presently on and where it joined the Clearwater River, which led to the Columbia River. He explained to Clark that they were only ten "sleeps" (or nights) to the falls of the Columbia River. Twisted Hair also told Clark that many Indians lived on the Columbia and they would find other white men at the great falls.

Lewis and Clark presented the chiefs with gifts of shirts, knives, tobacco, and the peace medals. Days later, the chiefs demanded more goods in exchange for more dried fish, camas roots, and berries. Lewis and Clark had no choice but to agree.

Making Canoes

While the Corps of Discovery stayed among the Nez Percé people, Chief Twisted Hair showed Clark how to make dugout canoes by burning them out of a tree. Clark and the few men who were not severely sick began the process of hollowing out and shaping five large ponderosa pine trees. Each tree was three to four feet (.9 to 1.2 m) in diameter.

Twisted Hair taught the men to lay a log over a fire trench until an area of wood turned to charcoal. The Indians would use stone axes and scrapers to chip out the charred wood. The Indian method was easier and produced a better canoe. The burning sealed the wood against insects and rot.

Clark also found this process was much faster. He and the men completed four large canoes and one smaller canoe in ten days.

The men continued to be ill from their new diet. For more than a week, the men were unable to travel. Most could barely move.

The Nez Percé discussed what should be done about the weak, sickly white men. It would have been easy to kill them and take their weapons. As the Indians considered their plan, one Nez Percé woman came forward and said, "These are the people who helped me. Do them no hurt."[7] Watkuweis had been captured by the Blackfeet Indians and sold in Canada to a white fur trader. After many years, she returned to her people. The kindness she had been shown by the white people in Canada saved the Corps.

While many of the men battled their illnesses, Clark and others made five canoes out of ponderosa pines. Chief Twisted Hair showed Clark the Indian method of slowly burning out the canoe instead of cutting it. He also offered to accompany the expedition downstream to assure other Indians that the white men came in peace.

On October 7, the Corps put the canoes into the water and set out. For the first time in two years, they traveled with the current.

Lost Trail in the Bitterroot Mountains

Beacon Rock on the Columbia River, where the men witnessed the effects of the tide for the first time

THE COLUMBIA RIVER AND FORT CLATSOP

The swift current of the Clearwater River carried the five canoes of the Corps of Discovery along at a quick pace. The men were weak, but recovering. They battled dangerous rapids but continued in the canoes instead of portaging.

The men were energized by their progress and anxious to make it to the ocean.

The dugout canoes were harder to handle and susceptible to overturning, leaking, and becoming swamped. But the men continued to chance the whitewater rapids in their pursuit of the Pacific. Old Toby was frightened of the rapids and left the expedition during the night without his pay.

The group traveled down the Clearwater to the junction with the Snake River. As they continued down the Snake River, they were met by Indians along the river's edge. Twisted Hair and Nez Percé Chief Tetoharsky had traveled ahead of the Corps to inform the Indians that white men in dugout canoes were coming in peace.

THE PACIFIC NORTHWEST

The expedition traded with the Yakima, Walla Walla, and the Wanapam for dogs to be killed for meat. Finally, they were able to eat something other than fish.

The Corps followed the Snake River into present-day Washington and into the dense Pacific Northwest rain forest. By October 16, 1805, the group knew they were getting close to the coast.

They had reached the Columbia River, which cut through the Cascade Mountains. They made camp and investigated the area. The crystal clear water of the Columbia River was teeming with salmon. Dense forests surrounded them, and hot, humid weather brought rain every day.

THE GREAT FALLS

On October 23, the Corps of Discovery came to the falls area of the Columbia River. For 55 miles (89 km), the river ran through falls and narrow channels and between high cliffs. Lewis and Clark agreed they would have to portage around one of the falls, a 20-foot (6-m) drop called Celilo Falls. They were helped by some local Indians. Elk-skin ropes were used to lower the canoes down the drop, while the Indians helped portage their supplies.

On October 24, the expedition came to a set of falls called The Dalles. A quarter-mile (0.4 km) stretch of rapids, called the Short Narrows, led up to the falls. The Indians informed the captains there was no way to canoe down the whitewater rapids and survive. Finding no way to portage the canoes, the captains agreed they would proceed. The men who could not swim carried the journals, rifles, ammunition, and scientific equipment across land. The natives gathered by the river to watch the foolish white men drown in the rapids. Miraculously, the party successfully ran the "impassable" rapids.

The explorers continued down the Columbia River and came to an Indian village of wooden homes, something they had not seen since 18 months earlier in St. Charles. The expedition stopped at this village of Chinook Indians. Twisted Hair and Tetoharsky stayed with the group for a few more days and then returned to their people.

During the first two days of November, the Corps continued on the Columbia River. As they moved downriver and past Beacon Rock, they noticed the water was rising and falling with the tide. They were getting closer to the ocean. The fog was thick and the rain constant.

They made their camp on November 2 near the mouth of the Willamette River near present-day Vancouver, Washington. This area had been previously explored by whites. The men were once again in country that already had been mapped.

Communication

The Corps of Discovery found the Chinook to be friendly and helpful. Communication was difficult, though. No one among the Corps spoke Chinookan, and these Indians did not use the sign language of the Plains tribes.

OCEAN IN VIEW!

Five days later, on the afternoon of November 7, the fog lifted and the group shouted for joy. Clark scribbled his famous words, "Ocian in view! O! the joy."[1] Despite the rain, the men's energy was restored. They began paddling harder.

That night, they heard the sound of waves. Clark determined the miles they had traveled and wrote, "Ocian 4142 Miles from the Mouth of Missouri R."[2] He was off by only approximately 40 miles (64 km).

THE MISERABLE RAIN

What the explorers had first believed to be the Pacific Ocean was actually a large bay. They were still 20 miles (32 km) from the coast. Strong rain forced them to stop, and they made camp. The men remained at their camp during 11 days of rain. On November 12, Clark wrote,

> It would be distressing to … See our Situation at this time all wet and cold … in a Cove Scercely large enough to Contain us … canoes at the mercy of the waves & driftwood … our party has been wet for 8 days ands is truly disagreeable.[3]

The waterlogged and cold men knew they were close to reaching their goal.

A beach at Cape Disappointment

Cape Disappointment

By November 15, the Corps was forced to set up camp on a sandy beach along the bay. Groups were sent out in search of food and settlements of white men on the coast. Lewis hoped to find European trading ships from which they could buy more supplies. There were none to be found. Joseph Whitehouse wrote, "Our officers named this Cape,

Cape disappointment, on account of not finding Vessells there."[4]

That same day, Lewis reached the Pacific Ocean. Three days later, Clark arrived. The two men looked out at the endless ocean. After 18 months, they had succeeded in reaching their journey's goal.

A Group Decision

On November 24, 1805, Captains Lewis and Clark called all the members of the party together. The Corps of Discovery voted to cross the Columbia River and spend the

A Monumental Vote

On November 24, 1805, the expedition reached the place where the Columbia River emptied into the Pacific Ocean. They also had an important decision to make: where to spend the winter of 1805–1806. They had the options of heading back upriver, staying on the north side of the Columbia River, or crossing to the south side of the river, where they were told elk were plentiful.

As military captains, Lewis and Clark could have made the decision on their own. However, they decided to put the decision to a vote. The captains counted and recorded the votes and each member's reasons—including York and Sacagawea. This was the first time in history that an African American was allowed to vote. It also was the first time a woman cast an official ballot. It was clearly important to Captains Lewis and Clark that each person have a vote in where the Corps would stay for the winter. The Corps chose to move to the site near present-day Astoria, Oregon, where they constructed Fort Clatsop.

In 1870, the Fifteenth Amendment conferred the right to vote for emancipated African Americans—65 years after York cast his vote. In 1920, U.S. women won the federal right to vote—115 years after Sacagawea cast her vote.

winter on the south side of the river where, reportedly, there were elk.

WINTER AT FORT CLATSOP

The men built a fort a few miles from the coast near present-day Astoria, Oregon. They named it Fort Clatsop, after the Indians who had helped them. They cut down trees to use for huts and constructed two long structures that were divided into separate quarters, or cabins. The enlisted men stayed in one row of cabins. The other row housed the captains, Charbonneau, Sacagawea, and her son. The men built a storeroom and a smokehouse that was approximately 50 square feet (5 sq m). They moved into their quarters just before Christmas.

The Corps spent the winter preparing for their journey home. Some of the men made salt from seawater. Others made candles, sewed clothes, and hunted elk and deer. Elk hides were scraped to make moccasins for the return trip.

Clothing for the Return Trip

The Corps of Discovery had left St. Louis dressed in military uniforms and civilian clothing. By the winter at Fort Clatsop, their clothes had worn out. They spent the winter sewing clothing for the return trip. These new clothes were far different from their previous ones. By now, they had adopted many of the American-Indians' styles of dress, including moccasins and leather clothing.

A Monstrous Creature

While at Fort Clatsop, the Corps learned that a whale had been washed ashore. A group was sent to obtain some of the blubber and oil to use for cooking. Sacagawea asked to join them. She was overjoyed to see both the ocean and such a monstrous creature.

Lewis and Clark spent the winter making notes about the expedition. Lewis drew sketches of birds and fish and recorded data of the animals and plants. Clark finished the first map drawn of the Pacific Northwest.

The conditions at Fort Clatsop were miserable. It rained nearly every day, men caught colds and influenza, and the hunters were not coming back with enough meat. Chinook and Clatsop Indians visited the fort almost daily. The captains traded for fish and roots but worried about running out of goods to trade during the return trip.

The men endured the months of relentless rain, terrible food, and chores at Fort Clatsop waiting for the spring, when they could finally travel east, toward home. ⌐

A replica of Fort Clatsop, where the expedition stayed during the winter of 1805–1806

Icy waters of the Columbia River

The Journey Home

On March 23, 1806, after three months at Fort Clatsop, the men packed up their canoes and headed east.

Paddling against the current of the Columbia River was hard work. The men were also followed by

Indians. One day a group of Indians stole Lewis's Newfoundland dog, Seaman. He sent a group of men after them and ordered that "if they made the least resistence or difficulty in surrendering the dog to fire on them."[1] The Indians returned the dog before shots were fired.

At Celilo Falls, the group opted to buy horses from the local Indians and travel over land instead of continuing on the river. They also purchased dogs to eat, as the hunting was poor. The Corps spent a few days among the Walla Wallas and Chief Yellept. Lewis wrote, "I think we can justly affirm to the honor of these people that they are the most hospitable, honest, and sincere people that we have met with in our voyage."[2]

Returning to the Nez Percé

The expedition continued eastward. By May, they had returned to Twisted Hair and the Nez Percé tribe who had kept and protected the expedition's horses. However, the snow was still too deep in the Bitterroots, and the men could not proceed. They stayed with the Nez Percé for weeks.

Clark treated the Nez Percé for ulcers, arthritis, and even paralysis. The Indians paid him with food, but it was not enough. Soon, the men discovered they could trade some of their clothes and buttons (especially brass buttons) for food supplies.

The men passed the time by competing in shooting matches and horse races with the Nez Percé. Lewis won the shooting match, but the young warriors bested the Americans in riding.

ATTEMPTING THE BITTERROOTS

On June 10, the men headed toward the Weippe Prairie and the Bitterroot Mountains. They had spent four weeks among the Nez Percé. Twisted Hair insisted the Lolo Trail would be too snowy to pass, but the Americans were restless to get going.

Despite the warnings of the Nez Percé, the Corps of Discovery attempted to cross the Bitterroots too early. Within a week, they were struggling to find the trail under 12 feet (4 m) of snow. Lewis wrote, "Here was winter with all it's rigors."[3] They had to turn around. Lewis wrote, "The party were a good deel dejected. ... This is the first time since we have been on this long tour that we have ever been compelled to retreat."[4]

They attempted to cross the Bitterroots again on June 24. Lewis and Clark had bartered two

rifles to gain the aid of young Nez
Percé guides to help them over the
Lolo Pass. Even though it was June,
they crossed over land covered with
several feet of snow and endured
cold temperatures. It was evident the
guides were capable.

On June 30, just six days after
starting out, the group reached
Travelers' Rest. The young Nez Percé
guides had led them for 165 miles
(266 km).

"If we proceeded and
should get bewildered in
these mountains the cer-
tainty was that we should
loose all our horses and
consequently our bag-
gage instruments perhaps
our papers and thus emi-
nently wrisk the loss of
the discoveries which we
had already made if we
should be so fortunate as
to escape with life."[5]
—Meriwether Lewis,
June 17, 1806

Separate Parties

With the rugged mountains behind them, Lewis
and Clark felt a sense of relief. Their confidence
was restored. They enacted a plan—the Corps of
Discovery was about to split up.

The captains wanted to explore more of the
Louisiana Territory to include in their report to
Jefferson. Perhaps there was an easier route to the
Pacific than the one they had taken. Lewis would
take nine men and seventeen horses and follow the
Nez Percé shortcut to the Great Falls of the Missouri
River. Once there, they would search for the mouth

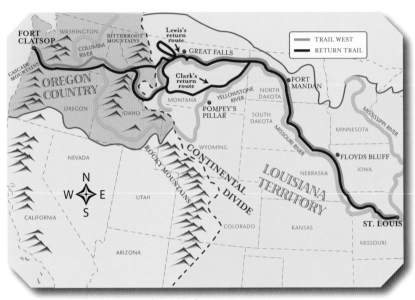

The expedition's journey
(present-day state names provided for reference)

of the Marias River. Lewis would head straight into the heart of Blackfeet Indian country, a tribe feared by many.

Clark and the rest of the group would head for the Lemhi Pass to retrieve the gear they had stored there the previous fall. That group would then split up. Sergeant Ordway would lead ten men back to the mouth of the Marias River. Clark would take the rest of the men, Sacagawea, and Jean-Baptiste from the Three Forks to the Yellowstone River. They would build canoes and paddle to where the Yellowstone met the Missouri River. There, most of the expedition's members would reunite.

The plan was a dangerous one. The smaller parties would be at a greater risk should they run into trouble with any Indians. But Lewis and Clark were confident of the men's abilities.

Words of Parting

As the Corps prepared to go their separate ways, Lewis wrote, "I took leave of my worthy friend and companion, Capt. Clark and the party that accompanyed him. I could not avoid feeling much concern on this occasion although I hoped this separation was only momentary."[6]

THE YELLOWSTONE RIVER

On July 3, the Corps split up. Clark's group had about 1,000 miles (1,609 km) to cover. Lewis and his men would travel about 800 miles (1,287 km). Both parties would be in unknown territory. Clark's group headed south and reached the Beaverhead River to recover the supplies they had stored the previous autumn. At this point, Sergeant Ordway took his men and headed downstream.

Clark's group headed east over land. They were now in Sacagawea's territory and she guided them through shortcuts and easier routes. They reached the Yellowstone River on July 15 and began making canoes. On July 19, they awoke to discover that half of their horses had been stolen in the night.

On July 24, Clark's group set off down the Yellowstone River. They passed enormous herds of game—buffalo, elk, antelopes, and wolves—all a welcome sight. The men were eager to eat something other than fish, horses, or dogs.

The following day, the group passed a large sandstone outcropping that Clark named Pompy's Tower, after Sacagawea's son. Clark stopped the canoes, climbed up the rock, and carved his name into the sandstone. Two hundred years later, the rock with Clark's name still remains.

The Marias Exploration

While Clark and his group headed down the Yellowstone River,

Firearms of the Expedition

Lewis and Clark's expedition brought a large collection of firearms into the West. The explorers felt it was important to keep these secure from the Indians so they would not use them against neighboring tribes.

Lewis obtained firearms for the expedition from Harpers Ferry, an armory in West Virginia. He collected 15 rifles, 24 large knives, powder horns, bullet molds, and 60 tomahawks.

The Model 1803 rifles were the standard issue for U.S. Army soldiers. With a range of up to 200 yards (183 m), the weapon was used to take down grizzlies and buffalo. Because Lewis had purchased only 15 rifles, the enlisted men brought their own Model 1795 muskets and bayonets. Additionally, there were numerous pistols, two blunderbusses, a fowler (for shooting birds), Charbonneau's gun, and Lewis and Clark's officer's swords.

John Shields acted as gunsmith, fixing and altering the guns and rifles when they needed it—which was often.

Captain Lewis headed for the Marias River. When his party reached the river, they split up. Lewis took Drouillard and the Field brothers to investigate the Marias River. As they proceeded, Lewis noticed eight Blackfeet Indians watching them. Uneasy, he met with them and gave them handkerchiefs and peace medals. He explained they had established trade with the Shoshone and Nez Percé and hoped to do the same with the Blackfeet. That night, Lewis and his three men camped with the Blackfeet.

Trouble with the Blackfeet Indians

Lewis awoke at first light to a skirmish. Joseph Field was fighting to keep his rifle, which a Blackfeet was attempting to steal. His brother Reubin had stabbed and killed one of the Indians in a fight over his rifle. Lewis discovered his rifle was gone as well. He drew his pistol and demanded his weapon be returned. The warrior dropped the gun.

Two of the Blackfeet Indians were in the process of stealing the

"I then drew a pistol from my holster and terning myself about saw the Indian making off with my gun. I ran at him with my pistol and bid him lay down my gun, which he was in the act of doing when the Fieldses returned and drew up their guns to shoot him, which I forbade as he did not appear to be about to make any resistance or commit any offensive act, He droped the gun and walked slowly off."[7]
—Meriwether Lewis,
July 27, 1806

explorers' horses. Lewis ran to stop them, shooting one who aimed a rifle at him. The Blackfeet was hit but returned fire, missing Lewis by inches. The remaining Blackfeet fled.

Lewis and his men were able to retrieve their rifles and horses, but two Blackfeet Indians were dead. Six of the tribesmen headed back to their camp, and Lewis feared more Indians would return. Lewis and his men mounted their horses and fled toward the Missouri River, riding hard for 24 hours. They covered 120 miles (193 km) to reach the Missouri River. In a stroke of fortune, they were met by part of the Corps of Discovery as they came around a bend in the river. It was August 12, and the expedition had been separated for five weeks. Lewis's group quickly climbed into the canoes. The reunited Corps of Discovery paddled hard down the Missouri River, trying to put as much distance between them and any Blackfeet who might be in pursuit.

Clark named this sandstone outcropping "Pompy's Tower," after Sacagawea's son. Clark also carved his name into the stone.

Chapter 10

HISTORY

OF

THE EXPEDITION

UNDER THE COMMAND OF

CAPTAINS LEWIS AND CLARK,

TO

THE SOURCES OF THE MISSOURI,

THENCE

ACROSS THE ROCKY MOUNTAINS

AND DOWN THE

RIVER COLUMBIA TO THE PACIFIC OCEAN.

PERFORMED DURING THE YEARS 1804—5—6.

By order of the

GOVERNMENT OF THE UNITED STATES.

The first published version of Lewis and Clark's notes from the expedition

HOME AGAIN

The Corps made good time on the Missouri River. They arrived at the Mandan villages on August 14, two days after they had met up with Clark's group at the Yellowstone River. Clark offered to raise Jean-Baptiste and provide him with a formal education. Sacagawea and Charbonneau agreed that when the boy was old enough, they would send him to live with Clark.

John Colter, one of the enlisted men, was granted an early discharge to return to the Yellowstone River to trap beavers. The remaining members of the Corps of Discovery made good progress down the Missouri River, covering up to 100 miles (161 km) on some days. They stopped at Charles Floyd's grave—the only member of the Corps of Discovery who did not survive the trip.

As they continued downriver, they began meeting boats of trappers and traders. They swapped news of the West for news from back home. Lewis, Clark, and the others were told that most people had assumed the members of the expedition were all dead. It had been more than two years since they had left.

BACK IN ST. LOUIS

On September 20, the Corps saw a sight they had not seen for more than two years—a cow grazing by the river. They were nearing home.

Finally, on September 23, 1806, the Corps of Discovery arrived in

"... rejoiced that we have the Expedition Completed ... we entend to return to our native homes to See our parents once more as we have been so long from them."[1]

—*John Ordway, September 23, 1806*

When the Corps of Discovery returned to St. Louis, Captain Lewis sent a few letters to Jefferson as a preliminary report. One letter read, "In obedience to your orders we have penetrated the continent of North America to the Pacific Ocean, and sufficiently explored the interior of the country to affirm with confidence that we have discovered the most practicable rout which does exist across the continent by means of the navigable branches of the Missouri and Columbia Rivers."[2]

After returning to St. Louis, Captain Lewis suffered from depression and did not take steps toward publishing the journals. After the death of Meriwether Lewis, William Clark traveled to Philadelphia to arrange the publication of the journals. Finally, in 1814, eight years after the Corps returned from the expedition, an edited synopsis of the journals were put into print, along with the map Clark had created while at Fort Clatsop.

St. Louis. The townsfolk lined the riverbanks to welcome them home. The men who had left in pursuit of the Northwest Passage to the Pacific Ocean had traveled approximately 8,000 miles (12,875 km) over two years and four months. They had done the impossible. They were national heroes.

AFTER THE EXPEDITION

The men collected their pay in St. Louis. Congress awarded each man double pay and 320 acres (129 ha) of land. Lewis and Clark were each awarded 1,600 acres (647 ha).

President Jefferson was eager to hear every detail of the trip. He had received the boxes the captains had sent back to St. Louis their first winter. But there was still much to learn from Lewis and Clark.

Meriwether Lewis faced new struggles after returning from the West. In March of 1807, he became governor of the Louisiana Territory. He drank heavily and incurred debts in explorations that he believed the U.S. government would reimburse. However, Congress refused to cover the nearly $4,000 that Lewis owed. In debt and suffering from depression, Meriwether Lewis took his life on October 11, 1809, at the age of 35. Three years earlier, he had returned from the most important discovery expedition in U.S. history.

William Clark became a brigadier general in the U.S. Army and Superintendent of Indian Affairs. He married Julia Hancock in 1808. Their

The Westward Journey Nickel Series

The year 2003 marked 200 years since the Corps of Discovery departed for their great expedition. The U.S. Mint commemorated the Lewis and Clark Bicentennial with the Westward Journey Nickel Series. From 2004 to 2006, the Jefferson nickel was modified and included images depicting the journey.

The 2004 series began with the release of the Peace Medal and Keelboat nickels. Like the peace medal Lewis and Clark presented to American-Indian chiefs as a token of peace and goodwill, the Peace Medal nickel depicts two clasped hands on one side and Jefferson's likeness on the other.

In 2005, the image on the back of the coin depicted a bison, or buffalo, for the first issue. The second issue included the inscription "Ocean in view! O! The joy!" with an image of the Pacific Ocean coast. The front of the 2005 nickel bears a profile of Jefferson's face and "Liberty" inscribed in Jefferson's handwriting.

The 2006 nickel depicts an updated image of Jefferson's home, Monticello, on the back. The front is a portrait of Jefferson accompanied by the "Liberty" inscription that was on the 2005 nickel.

son, Meriwether Lewis Clark, was born in 1809.
Sacagawea and Charbonneau brought Jean-Baptiste
to St. Louis in 1809. The Clarks adopted him and
provided him with an education. In 1813, Clark
became governor of the Missouri Territory. In 1814,
he oversaw the editing of a two-volume version of
the journals he and Lewis had kept. At the age of 68,
William Clark died on September 1, 1838, in St.
Louis at his son's home.

York

After returning from the expedition, York was once again Clark's slave. He asked for his freedom, but Clark did not grant him that request. However, in 1809, he did allow York to move to Kentucky to be close to his wife, who had a different owner.

More than ten years after they returned from the West, Clark granted York his freedom. York entered the freighting business in Kentucky and Tennessee. It is believed that York died of cholera before 1832.

An Expedition of Enormous Proportions

Although Meriwether Lewis
and William Clark never found the
Northwest Passage, they introduced
172 new plants and 122 new animals
to science. They encountered as many
as 100 American-Indian tribes and
helped to establish trade relations
with them. They mapped land west
of the Mississippi River. Most of all,
they charted the course for a nation
expanding into a land rich with
resources and possibilities. ⌐

Bronze monument depicting Lewis and Clark with Sacagawea

TIMELINE

1803

Jefferson asks Lewis to lead a search for the Northwest Passage. Lewis asks William Clark to be his cocaptain.

1804

Led by Lewis and Clark, the Corps of Discovery leaves Camp Dubois on May 14 and sets out up the Missouri River.

1804

On July 4, the Corps celebrates the first Independence Day west of the Mississippi River.

1805

The keelboat is sent back to St. Louis on April 7. Charbonneau, Sacagawea, and their baby son join the expedition.

1805

On May 5, Lewis and another member of the Corps kill the first grizzly bear to be scientifically described.

1805

On June 13, the men begin an 18-mile (29-km) portage around the Great Falls of the Missouri River.

1804

Lewis and Clark meet with the Oto and Missouri tribes on August 3.

1804

On August 20, Charles Floyd dies near present-day Sioux City, Iowa. He is the only fatality.

1804

In late October, the Corps reaches the Mandan and Hidatsa villages, where they spend the winter.

1805

On August 12, Lewis ascends the Continental Divide and sees the Rocky Mountains the Corps will have to cross.

1805

Lewis and Clark negotiate for horses with the Shoshone Indians on August 17.

1805

The expedition endures a blizzard in the Bitterroot Mountains in September.

TIMELINE

1805	1805	1806
Lewis and Clark reach the Pacific Ocean in November.	The men build Fort Clatsop, where they spend the winter.	The Corps of Discovery leaves Fort Clatsop on March 23 and begins the journey home.

1806	1807	1809
The Corps of Discovery paddles into St. Louis, Missouri, on September 23 after a journey of more than two years.	Lewis becomes governor of the Louisiana Territory.	Lewis dies near Nashville, Tennessee, on October 11. His death is ruled a suicide.

1806

On July 3, the Corps splits into smaller groups to explore more territory.

1806

The smaller groups of the Corps are reunited at the mouth of the Yellowstone River on August 12.

1806

The expedition arrives at Mandan on August 14 and takes leave of Charbonneau, Sacagawea, and Jean-Baptiste.

1813

Clark is named governor of the Missouri Territory.

1838

On September 1, Clark dies in St. Louis, Missouri, at the age of 68.

ESSENTIAL FACTS

DATE OF EVENT

May 14, 1804 to September 23, 1806

PLACES OF EVENT

❖ Fort Dubois, Missouri: the Corps of Discovery's point of departure journeying upriver

❖ Council Bluff, Nebraska: met Oto and Missouri tribe members

❖ South Dakota: entered Teton Sioux territory

❖ Knife River, North Dakota: met Mandan and Hidatsa

❖ Mandan, North Dakota: built a winter fort; hired Sacagawea and Charbonneau as interpreters

❖ Continental Divide: reached this mountainous ridge that separates the direction in which rivers in North America flow; rivers west of the divide flow into the Pacific Ocean; the Corps could now paddle downriver with the current

❖ Bitterroot Mountains: expedition became lost in a snowstorm; men became weak and ill

❖ Pacific Ocean: the Corps reached the Pacific Ocean after a river and land journey of more than 4,200 miles (6,760 km)

❖ Fort Clatsop, Oregon coast: built a fort for the winter and prepared for the return trip

KEY PLAYERS

❖ Thomas Jefferson

❖ Meriwether Lewis

❖ William Clark

❖ The men of the Corps of Discovery

❖ Sacagawea

❖ Various Indian tribes

HIGHLIGHTS OF EVENT

The goal of the expedition was to find a water passage or route that connected the Atlantic Ocean on the east side of the nation to the Pacific Ocean on the west. While no such passage was found, the Corps of Discovery was successful in other ways.

❖ The explorers encountered as many as 100 American-Indian tribes. They also were able to establish trade relations with many of the tribes.

❖ The expedition documented the geography, the resources, and the people they encountered.

❖ The expedition documented nearly 200 new plant species and more than 100 animals new to science.

QUOTE

"I took leave of my worthy friend and companion, Capt. Clark and the party that accompanyed him. I could not avoid feeling much concern on this occasion although I hoped this separation was only momentary."—*Meriwether Lewis, July 3, 1806*

ADDITIONAL RESOURCES

SELECT BIBLIOGRAPHY

Ambrose, Stephen E. *Undaunted Courage: Meriwether Lewis, Thomas Jefferson, and the Opening of the American West.* New York: Simon & Schuster, 1996.

Hamilton, John C. *Lewis & Clark: Adventures West. An Illustrated Journey.* Eden Prairie, MN: Sparrow Media Group, 2004.

Lewis, Meriwether and William Clark. *The Journals of Lewis and Clark.* Ed. Bernard DeVoto. New York: Houghton Mifflin Company, 1981.

Lewis & Clark: The Journey of the Corps of Discovery. Dir. Ken Burns. PBS. 12 Mar. 2007 <http://www.pbs.org/lewisandclark/>.

FURTHER READING

Blumberg, Rhoda. *York's Adventures with Lewis and Clark: An African American's Part in the Great Expedition.* New York: Harper Collins Publishers, 2004.

Hamilton, John. *The Corps of Discovery.* Edina, MN: ABDO & Daughters, 2003.

Webster, Christine. *The Lewis and Clark Expedition.* New York: Children's Press, 2003.

Web Links

To learn more about the Lewis and Clark expedition, visit ABDO Publishing Company on the World Wide Web at **www.abdopublishing.com**. Web sites about the Lewis and Clark expedition are featured on our Book Links page. These links are routinely monitored and updated to provide the most current information available.

Places to Visit

Fort Clatsop National Memorial
92343 Fort Clatsop Road, Astoria, OR 97103
503-861-2471
http://www.nps.gov.focl
View a reconstruction of the fort near its original site and demonstrations of frontier skills the Corps used.

Fort Mandan
838 28th Avenue Southeast, Washburn, ND 58577-0607
701-462-8535
http://www.fortmandan.org
Visit a reconstruction of Fort Mandan, where the Corps of Discovery spent their first winter.

Lewis and Clark National Historic Trail Interpretive Center
4201 Giant Springs Road, Great Falls, MT 59403
406-727-8733
http://www.fs.fed.us/r1/lewisclark/lcic.htm
The museum features exhibits detailing the expedition and American-Indian culture.

Pompeys Pillar National Monument
25 miles east of Billings, MT
406-875-2233
http://www.mt.blm.gov/pillarmon/general.html
Location of the pillar where Clark's carved signature can still be seen in the sandstone.

Glossary

blunderbuss
A firearm with a short barrel that is muzzle loaded.

bow
The front of a boat.

brigadier general
An officer in the Army who ranks above a colonel.

cache
To hide or store something.

chronometer
A device, much like a clock, used for calculating time.

Continental Divide
The point at which all water in North America flows either east to the Atlantic Ocean or west to the Pacific Ocean.

expedition
A journey taken with a specific purpose.

interpreter
A person who translates languages.

keelboat
A shallow, flat-bottomed boat that can be rowed, poled, or pulled from shore.

latitude
A point on the earth's surface measured in relation to how far north or south it is from the equator.

longitude
A point on the earth's surface measured in relation to how far east or west it is from the Prime Meridian.

mess
A group of men, led by a sergeant, who would perform tasks as a unit.

Northwest Passage
A water route that runs overland to connect the Atlantic and Pacific Oceans.

pirogue
> A boat similar to a canoe in shape and size.

portage
> To carry supplies and boats overland from one body of water to another.

posthumously
> Following or occurring after death.

ration
> An allocated amount of food.

specimen
> A sample used as an example or for testing purposes.

stern
> The back of a boat.

survey
> To use mathematical instruments to determine location.

swivel gun
> A small cannon.

tallow
> A waxy, white fat used to make candles and soap.

teem
> To be in large quantities; overflowing.

treaty
> An agreement made between two governments.

vermilion
> A bright, reddish-orange color.

SOURCE NOTES

Chapter 1. Into the Unknown

1. John C. Hamilton. *Lewis & Clark: Adventures West.* An Illustrated Journey. Eden Prairie, MN: Sparrow Media Group, 2004. 114.

2. Stephen E. Ambrose. *Undaunted Courage: Meriwether Lewis, Thomas Jefferson, and the Opening of the American West.* New York: Simon & Schuster, 1996. 101.

3. National Park Service. "The Lewis and Clark Journey of Discovery." 10 Oct. 2007 <http://www.nps.gov/archive/jeff/ LewisClark2/CorpsOfDiscovery/Preparing/Preparing.htm>.

4. Stephen E. Ambrose. *Undaunted Courage: Meriwether Lewis, Thomas Jefferson, and the Opening of the American West.* New York: Simon & Schuster, 1996. 79.

Chapter 2. Preparing for an Expedition

1. *Discovering Lewis & Clark.* VIAs, Inc. 20 Apr. 2007 <http://www. lewis-clark.org>.

2. *Lewis & Clark: The Journey of the Corps of Discovery.* PBS. 12 Mar. 2007 <http://www.pbs.org/lewisandclark/inside/gdrou.html>.

Chapter 3. The Exploration Begins

1. Meriwether Lewis and William Clark. *The Journals of Lewis and Clark.* Ed. Bernard DeVoto. New York: Houghton Mifflin Company, 1981. 308–309.

2. Ibid. 425–426.

3. Ibid. 8.

4. Stephen E. Ambrose. *Undaunted Courage: Meriwether Lewis, Thomas Jefferson, and the Opening of the American West.* New York: Simon & Schuster, 1996. 149.

Chapter 4. Among the Indians

1. Meriwether Lewis and William Clark. *The Journals of Lewis and Clark.* Ed. Bernard DeVoto. New York: Houghton Mifflin Company, 1981. 16.

2. Ibid.

3. Ibid. 21.

4. Ibid. 72.

5. Ibid. 256–257.

Chapter 5. Westward Bound

1. Stephen E. Ambrose. *Undaunted Courage: Meriwether Lewis, Thomas Jefferson, and the Opening of the American West.* New York: Simon & Schuster, 1996. 210.
2. Ibid. 217.
3. Ibid.
4. Ibid. 219.
5. Ibid. 220.

Chapter 6. Crossing the Continental Divide

1. Stephen E. Ambrose. *Undaunted Courage: Meriwether Lewis, Thomas Jefferson, and the Opening of the American West.* New York: Simon & Schuster, 1996. 264.
2. Ibid. 265.
3. Ibid. 266.
4. Meriwether Lewis and William Clark. *The Journals of Lewis and Clark.* Ed. Bernard DeVoto. New York: Houghton Mifflin Company, 1981. 189.
5. Ibid. 191.
6. Stephen E. Ambrose. *Undaunted Courage: Meriwether Lewis, Thomas Jefferson, and the Opening of the American West.* New York: Simon & Schuster, 1996. 284.
7. Meriwether Lewis and William Clark. *The Journals of Lewis and Clark.* Ed. Bernard DeVoto. New York: Houghton Mifflin Company, 1981. 206.

Chapter 7. Crossing the Mountains

1. Stephen E. Ambrose. *Undaunted Courage: Meriwether Lewis, Thomas Jefferson and the Opening of the American West.* New York: Simon & Schuster, 1996. 289.
2. Ibid 291.
3. Meriwether Lewis and William Clark. *The Journals of Lewis and Clark.* Ed. Bernard DeVoto. New York: Houghton Mifflin Company, 1981. 233.
4. Ibid. 239–240.
5. Stephen E. Ambrose. *Undaunted Courage: Meriwether Lewis, Thomas Jefferson and the Opening of the American West.* New York: Simon & Schuster, 1996. 295.

Source Notes Continued

6. Meriwether Lewis and William Clark. *The Journals of Lewis and Clark.* Ed. Bernard DeVoto. New York: Houghton Mifflin Company, 1981. 241.

7. Stephen E. Ambrose. *Undaunted Courage: Meriwether Lewis, Thomas Jefferson, and the Opening of the American West.* New York: Simon & Schuster, 1996. 300.

Chapter 8. The Columbia River and Fort Clatsop

1. Stephen E. Ambrose. *Undaunted Courage: Meriwether Lewis, Thomas Jefferson, and the Opening of the American West.* New York: Simon & Schuster, 1996. 310.

2. Ibid.

3. Ibid. 313.

4. John C. Hamilton. *Lewis & Clark: Adventures West.* An Illustrated Journey. Eden Prairie, MN: Sparrow Media Group, 2004. 140.

Chapter 9. The Journey Home

1. Stephen E. Ambrose. *Undaunted Courage: Meriwether Lewis, Thomas Jefferson, and the Opening of the American West.* New York: Simon & Schuster, 1996. 355.

2. Ibid. 359.

3. Ibid. 371.

4. Meriwether Lewis and William Clark. *The Journals of Lewis and Clark.* Abr. Anthony Brandt. Washington, D.C.: National Geographic Society, 2002. 342.

5. Ibid. 159.

6. John C. Hamilton. *Lewis & Clark: Adventures West.* An Illustrated Journey. Eden Prairie, MN: Sparrow Media Group, 2004. 154.

7. Meriwether Lewis and William Clark. *The Journals of Lewis and Clark.* Ed. Bernard DeVoto. New York: Houghton Mifflin Company, 1981. 438.

Chapter 10. Home Again

1. Lewis & Clark: *The Journey of the Corps of Discovery.* PBS. 12 Mar. 2007 <http://www.pbs.org/lewisandclark/inside/mlewi.html>.

2. Ibid.

INDEX

Index Continued

ABOUT THE AUTHOR

Susan E. Hamen is an editor at a publishing company and is a freelance writer and editor for a variety of publications. This is her second children's book. Hamen lives in Minnesota with her husband and their young daughter and son. In her spare time, she enjoys reading, traveling, and camping. She has shared many miles of paddling and portaging Minnesota's northern woods with her dad and brothers.

PHOTO CREDITS

Montana Historical Society, Edward S. Paxson, cover, 3, 41; Blue Lantern Studio/Corbis, 6, 97 (bottom); AP Images, 13, 51, 96 (top); Connie Ricca/Corbis, 14, 37, 70, 75, 89, 99 (top); Comstock/Corbis, 21; Missouri Bankers Association, L. Edward Fisher, 22; North Wind Photo Archives, 29, 61, 90, 95, 99 (bottom); Bettmann/Corbis, 30, 42, 47, 96 (bottom), 97 (top); Nati Harnik/AP Images, 34; Mark A. Duncan/AP Images, 52; David Muench/Corbis, 62, 69; Don Ryan/AP Images, 79, 98 (top); Craig Tuttle/Corbis, 80